TIKKI TIKKI MAN

Caroline Carver

Ward Wood Publishing
www.wardwoodpublishing.co.uk

Published by Ward Wood Publishing
6 The Drive
Golders Green
London NW11 9SR
www.wardwoodpublishing.co.uk

The right of Caroline Carver to be identified as author
of this work has been asserted by her in accordance
with the Copyright, Designs and Patent Act, 1988.
Copyright © 2012 Caroline Carver
ISBN: 978-0-9568969-4-0

British Library Cataloguing in Publication Data. A CIP
record for this book can be obtained from the British
Library.

Designed and typeset in Palatino Linotype by
Ward Wood Publishing.
Cover design by Mike Fortune-Wood.
Cover photo by: Beltsazar
Storm in Tropical Island
Supplied by Dreamstime.com

Printed and bound in Great Britain by
Imprint Digital, Seychelles Farm,
Upton Pyne, Exeter, Devon EX5 5HY, UK

for Gabriel and the Wyverns of Orta
with my love

CONTENTS

Notes

I   ILLUSORY CITY   9

II   MAIA   17

III   SOLITUDE   53

POSTSCRIPT   63

About the Author

Acknowledgements

Notes

p.9 The legend of The Illusory City is shown in a painting in Cave 217 of the Dunhuang Mogao Grottoes on China's Silk Road.

p.20 An apple tree near Almaty in Southern Kazakhstan is thought to be the sole ancestor of most cultivars of the domesticated apple (Malus domestica).

p.63 The towers were built to collect pigeon dung which has a high nitrogen content enriched by phosphorus.

TIKKI TIKKI MAN

I   ILLUSORY CITY

a doorway
built
not by Eastern fingers
but the concentrated thoughts
of every mind   whose words
are still remembered
leads me
through a shower
of falling stars and meteors
until   I'm there

Open Sesame

a night wind blowing on my face
the desert empty around me

there's a child ahead of me
no   many children

one comes up
puts her hand in mine

– are there men in your city –   she asks
– are there chat rooms?

are there winkles crawling in and out of caves
slimy trails?

pale white worms?   sea-urchins
with black bristles?

are there pictures?
fingers poking in and out of holes

stuffed bears with crafty faces

do you know the Tikki Tikki Man?

can you hear the sound of muffled oars
as the boat rows upriver? –

this child got imagination
like midnight mushroom
talk too much
wordy as wing-clip parrot
strutting in hibiscus bush

dont pay no attention to her
or you rot your brain

– it's as close as you get to heaven –
says the storyteller

as the silhouette of the city
rises before us

>1001 turrets and winged pagoda roofs
>poised for flight

>rooms so large
>you can't see from one end to the other

>walls hidden
>behind living ferns   falling water

there are playgrounds and gardens for children
but why are they afraid?

– listen –   says the storyteller
– a group of treasure-seekers go to the desert

looking for a city
with a storehouse of jewels

but the trip is so difficult   so dangerous
they want to give up and go back

their leader uses his magical powers
to create an illusion

of this place they're looking for
and the travellers go forward with joy

as they catch their first glimpse of the city
beyond low hills

they believe they've arrived
at their destination

(why would they not believe this?)

The Illusory City's set at the foot
of The Heavenly Mountains

close by are low hills
streams splashing among boulders
and a broad river
winding its way down into the valley
where the travellers
rest themselves and their horses
in the shade of wild orchards
of plum and cherry
before making their way into the castle
whose bleak walls
contradict the comforts inside

in the great hall
there are a thousand roses

fragrance hangs in the air
with the sharp clarity of glaciers

monks with clasped hands
bow in greeting

      Namaste

Buddha is serene on his dais
silence is king

and although the road the treasure-seekers have taken
has been difficult

looking back
everything seems as green as summer pasture

they want to give the city a name
Xanadu perhaps   or Nirvana   Paradise

but afterwards they simply talk
of The Illusory City

what do they do in this place?

rest   feast
sleep in chambers hung with silk
on beds   thoughtful as clouds
so it feels as if they're flying
to an even greater heaven
on the backs of winter geese

each morning when they walk in the hills
visit the stables
where their horses are tended

they feel like gods

each morning they ask their leader
– where is the treasure kept?
when may we open the vaults and carry it away? –

– will we have to kill the peaceful monks
in order to take it from them? –

they are no longer sure
they can do this

but this is a place   where
like the world outside
autumn follows
the benevolence of summer days

as soon as they are well
their leader makes the city disappear
but the road ahead
still seems easy and welcoming

they've forgotten the rough stones
on the long roads travelled
which they must now travel again

as they turn their horses' heads
back into barren
unforgiving landscapes

through granite gorges
whose smooth enclosing walls
hide bandits   fever-givers   mountain lions

sometimes their horses die under them
as they pass through desert
where there is no water   no oasis
only a scent of death on the wind

– will they reach the fortress of gold? –
I ask the storyteller
– will they kill the inhabitants
take the treasure
rape and pillage   put men to the sword
the monks to women   the city to fire? –

II   MAIA

– he showed me letters –   she says
– he said they wrote
asking him to do it again
his cabin was lined with photographs

we're sitting in the bay window
of her father's house in Jamaica
the sun driving its way in
past ups and downs of the branches
of our favourite climbing tree

and though we've been friends for a while
she hasn't yet told me what he did to her

today her father's having a party
for his newfound friend
the Tikki Tikki Man
and we're in trouble
because we won't speak to him

– if your mother were alive
she'd send you to your room
for bad behaviour –

his grief's made him a man of stone
we can't reach him

– they're just children –
says the indulgent Tikki Tikki Man

he's the sly one
he wears his devil tail
at the front

soon we're tumbling round together
his hands slip slopping with kindness

as they stray over the places
where our breasts will come

a storm of guilt fills our minds
it's like chasing a herd of cows down the hill
part of us can't stop
part of us wants to know more

the Tikki Tikki Man
is a professional
opening new doors
one by one

– you must come again soon –
says her father
– while your ship's still in –

our world's a desert
we flick our fingers
and our horses come to us

we ride bareback   that's the best way
tell them our secrets
until they sigh through their wide nostrils

a great wind gathers itself up like a djinn
and roars away into the first evening
of the first day

you're on a magic carpet
looking down
and suddenly
there's an apple right below you

glowing bright and dim
on/off   on/off
and you think   *hey hey hey*
as you tip sideways

while the carpet

(oriental of course
all subdued and welcoming
reds and yellows
given you by a strangely hooded man
from the soukh in Baghdad)

drifts into a gentle turn
like a honey buzzard
navigating its way downwards

to a forest –
pine trees
the remains of ancient orchards

– *hey hey hey* –   says the carpet
producing its scientific credentials
as it settles on
a small landing place
by the banks of a secret river
near the path of the old Silk Road
through Kazakhstan

– take this one –   it says
– your man will love it –

being Bluebeard
means submarines

doors clanging shut
sonic booms   furtive night messengers

means sealing of fire   water   wind
reduction by earth and its dark shovels

watch out man   I see you slipping in and out
of corridors   look like rats got your face

your name mean

gnomes hiding gold
hard-core fires of Vesuvius

secrets wailing in concrete bunkers
crying unsafe   unsafe   in earthquakes

try go down into the volcano
come back when no one looking

there's a word out there
wrapped in deep space wrappings

flapping its wings like it just come
from the crack of doom

whisper-tracks of Concorde crisscross the sky
rattle windows

cry   *let me in   let me in*

even uncles can draw you onto their laps
and some wear their tails
at the front

secrets lie heavy in our saddlebags
Alma has filled them with sandwiches
sent us off into the woods

when we get there
the sandwiches have gone

and in their place
stones from the volcano

Maia holds to everything she knows
like a suit of armour

her world's made of granite
there's nothing else to learn
she's lost her curiosity

if I wonder why flowers open in the morning
and shut again at night

or ask why some burst out with great breaths of joy
filling us with the scent of mangoes and wild honey
and then hold it in again for weeks

she looks at her fingers
as if they've only just grown on her hands this morning

she turns her eyes away as she talks

– perhaps when I'm grown up
I'll stop remembering –   she says

we no longer climb trees
to spy on the world from our leafy hideaways

peep through half-open bedroom doors
stand on the beach wondering why the horizon
is always the same distance away
whether we are rowing our boat out to the reef
or standing on the ferry as it heads out to sea

when I persuade her to start riding again
she's like a sleep-walker
a stone-like calm on her face

– even weeds are stronger than I am –
she says   – I'm not like them
I don't want to push through concrete
I don't want to find the light –

Maia's mother
used to fill the house with roses

at night
when everyone had gone to bed

we'd pretend we were in a Sultan's garden

on an island   where there was never any light
except from the moon

the roses were pale as swans in mist
their scent filled all the spaces

sometimes we go to the kitchens
where we're not supposed to go
but everyone else is out
and today Maia cut herself when she fell off the donkey

the cook has also cut his arm
he picks her up
presses his dark skin against her freckles

– see   we're blood brother and sister –   he says
– we're the same under the skin –

we both love him as deeply
as we've ever loved anyone

but this was before the Tikki Tikki Man

spare me now!
everyone know this tale

it that tired old chestnut
pulled from the fire
every turning day

in the bath
Alma scrubs her back

Maia says her polished arms are the arms of a goddess
as she pulls her down to kiss her

she's sitting with her legs wide apart
only her knees show above the water

– see   I'm lots of islands –   she says
– I'm an archipelago –
(she learned this word yesterday)

– no chile   you all of a piece –   says Alma
– you a whole country –

she points between Maia's legs
– soon come tree and forest

a river of blood going flow down there one day –

she doesn't want any part of her body
to go missing

when she cuts her fingernails
she saves each new horn of a second moon

in a waterproof box
where they lie

like scales
of transparent fish

she hasn't cut her mermaid hair
since she was 12 years old

if she ever does   she says
it will join the fingernails

weaving calypso rhythms
into filaments of silk

we're playing at her house
when there's a knock on the door

it's the Tikki Tikki Man
but her father's not here

when he comes in
the scent of roses is replaced
by the prickle of Old Spice aftershave

we run into the garden
climb the mango tree

he's too fat to come after us

prowls round the base
like an angry wolf

there are days of happiness
sometimes we ride into the desert
well   it's really the beach

      soon we're cantering along the sand
the horses throwing up their heels
pretending to be colts again

they want to lie down and roll on their backs
but we take their bridles
coax them into the water
ride in the shallows
till the sea draws us into itself

– you see   horses   it's best here –   we say

but the Tikki Tikki Man has closed
so many doors to us

we're shipwrecked
on this outcrop of seashell and reef
only aurelia aurita
the slow white jellyfish
doesn't seem to mind

her pale calm reminds us
she's named for the moon

but I'm afraid for her
there's no food
and it's six hours till the tide comes back

like a woman with a bucket
daylight draws water from her shallow pool

        the sun moves slowly

aurelia's pale blue orifices
open and shut   open and shut

like the questing mouths of new babies
not sure which way to turn
in their self-contained worlds

– I'll never have children –   says Maia
as we wait for the lifeboat
nudging its way in among sharp rocks
so it can throw a line to us

the Tikki Tikki Man has gone back to his ship
we wrap our guilt into small bundles
hide them in cupboards
hope cockroaches will find and eat them

Maia says God is turning the world into sheet metal
taking painting lessons

outlining trees and bushes with a black brush
emptying the sea of its reflections

birds and butterflies disappear
and nobody sings   nobody sings

perhaps they've all got headaches

houses line up for the firing-squad
as men hammer plywood over their eyes

and the horses want to be invisible
jumping about and smashing their flanks against each other

until there's only one place for them to go
and that's the hurricane shelter

although it's full of hornets
who aren't about to bow off-stage like everyone else

for the next two days   the hurricane
and perhaps God as well   rip the island apart

until they're both tired of this and go north
taking that terrible all-seeing eye

those little shudders and quakes
the floods   armies of crabs   infestations of rats

and suddenly the air's fresh as a new-made photograph
even horses and birds and insects are happy again

so many ships have sunk in the bay
people are afraid to go fishing

sometimes we talk about God
there's a sign above the cemetery saying
'the peace of God that passeth all understanding'

we don't understand but it makes us
roll about laughing

we imitate the Tikki Tikki Man
lisping his way through it

we buy tamarind balls in the market
before we go to the beach

but we're not comfortable with the sight of men
in bulging bathing-suits

one of them scratches himself
and dark hairs creep into the sunlight

everything to do with men's bodies
has a bad feeling to it

the sweet sour taste of the tamarind balls
prickles our mouths

we're standing at the edge of a cliff
our backs to all the safe places
and Maia's father is full of pain

we listen with our blank faces
as he tells us off for always being rude
to his new friend   the Tikki Tikki Man

– don't you think I've got enough
unhappiness in my life already?

don't we all need friends?
he brings you wonderful presents –   he says
– when his ship comes in –

he says we're dumb as the island goats
perching on little rocks at the side of the road

the Tikki Tikki Man
brings photographs
shows them to us
when we're alone

afterwards
when he goes to the bathroom
I hide one of them
under the sofa

– your father says I can take you on the ship
for a visit –   he says

– I know you'd like to show your friend
what fun we have –

that night I ask if Maia can stay at my house
I tell her   she must be as brave as her pony was
when a mongoose ran out in front of it

she must tell her father about the Tikki Tikki Man

she starts to cry
says he won't believe her

I show her the photograph

when we go back to Maia's house
the Tikki Tikki Man
is waiting to take us to the ship

– now – I say to Maia

– now   now   now
now now now   N O W ! –

I take the Tikki Tikki Man into the garden
tell him that if we can go tomorrow
instead of today
I'll have something special to show him
I even fling my hips about
in what I think is a grown-up way

when we come back
Maia's in the study with her father
and the door is shut

when you're asleep your breath
moves more slowly
ghosting down mountains
like a nightdress without a person

this breath
is like fretted water
creeping over crushed oyster shells

until it catches you in nightmare
diving deep into forbidden places

and you wake gasping for air

when breathing is most shallow
the body pretends to rearrange itself
dividing its atoms
into new and peculiar arrangements

so next time you surface
the mind's playful with you   asking

          – where am I today?
is this the same body
we went to sleep in last night? –

there's been a trial
and now he's gone to prison for two years

Maia's sent to Paris
to stay with one of her aunts

she sees Tikki Tikki men everywhere

when she goes on the Metro
she disguises herself as an old woman

she says her father
will never smile again

man you is stiffer than Mount Rushmore
even if I climb with hammer of Thor
can't make no difference
your smile gone some other place

don't show your feelings man
might split your face

some days you remember
swimming along the reef
fish touching your legs   arms   even your lips
promising they'll never forget you

their morning colours
sing of market day
wild parrots   hummingbirds   little toddies
a crush of warm excitement
headdresses blue   red   purple   green

when the Tikki Tikki Man
comes out   he goes to Africa

we read timetables   check flight schedules
consider bombs

– you haven't seen the last of me –   he'd shouted
as the policemen took him away

Maia's in a hotel in Canada
her father's arranged a job for her
taking notes of meetings

she's the only woman among five hundred men
who make their living in the world of boxing

they treat her like one of their own children
gently   as if she's in a western movie
saved from what they'd call
'a fate worse than death'

they don't know that if they are to help her
they must swim to the tropical island
where she spends her nights

under a mango tree
hiding from the Tikki Tikki Man

Maia touches her pony as if she's one herself
its short coarse hair rippling like wind ruffling water

she currycombs   adjusts the bridle of lamp wick
her mother made for her

we lean our cheeks against warm flanks
waiting for a head to turn in our direction

waiting for the warming breath
the snort of recognition

Maia never talks about her mother

her father's sent her to stay
in a hotel in Scotland

and now she's alone with a stranger
for only the second time in her life

he tells her
his body's used in the pictures
on cereal packages

but his mother says
that when they put it together
they must use someone else's head
on top of his fine muscular body
or her neighbours will get
the wrong idea

he takes Maia to the barn
at the edge of a field
beyond the hotel
and plays his bagpipes to her

his kilt swirls round him
the sporran taps and bangs against his body

Maia admires the dirk wedged into his sock
his rugged Scottish calves   .

thinks of the Tikki Tikki Man
(there's no day
she does not think of him)

she wonders whether she can trust this Scot
who's lost among his bagpipes
as her father's lost in his books

she watches the in and out bag
which holds all his breath
and then lets it out again
like a valley wind

he seems good   innocent   kind
she'd like to meet his mother
but perhaps he wears the sporran
so no one will know
he has a tail at the front

– if you wear your hair like that –
says her neighbour
– someone's going to rape you –

Maia goes home and looks at herself in the mirror

she takes the kitchen scissors
hacks at the hair which reaches to her waist
tears it from her head till her scalp's bleeding
cuts the great swag away from herself
like a scythe of late summer wheat
trims   more slowly now
back to the fluff of childhood

then   gathering every last strand into a bag
she takes it out into the garden   sets fire to it

she'd thanked him for his thoughtfulness
now   she sees
he was warning her against himself

for the next seven weeks
the smell of burning hair stays with her

she never goes out

each night she dreams of a forest in flames
animals running into the desert
bodies singed with pain
radiating a terrible light

where this nonsense come from
why she think she so special?
soon she say

– why don you like this unicorn
lying like sweet innocence
head in my lap? –

this babe got delusions man
long time since she been virgin

Only the owl sees how I sleep
under the pomegranate tree
woven into an embroidered garden
of forget-me-nots and campion

she has unmaidenly hands
she's put a chain round my neck
pulls at my mane
sings courtly music into my ears

Merde! je suis une licorne sérieuse mais
je deviendrai un poème polisson!

I'm supposed to be a legend of innocence
but I've slept too long

she's desperate for love
if I lay my head in her lap she'll undo me

III   SOLITUDE

we're going on a canoe expedition

Maia's psychiatrist thinks she must learn
to believe in goodness

her guru says   The Illusory City
will always be there for us

we've turned the back room of her apartment into a refuge
hung pictures of the city on its walls

each time we leave
we double lock the doors

some evenings we read love stories to each other
but they always end sadly

what these girls thinking?
the Tikki Tikki Man
move through walls and doorways
easy as shadow water

Rainer Maria Rilke says
love is when two solitudes meet and touch and greet each other

and we're going into the wilderness
with my boyfriend

and someone he knows called Marc
who's a trainee doctor

we're going with two canoes
two tents two *wanagans*

one for all our cooking things
the other for bedding

we carry packs on our backs
with the food in them

so we can hang them from branches at night
to be safe from bears

but on the first night
it's a porcupine

that clanks up a tree to investigate
sounding like a bag of metallic knitting needles

I'm hoping for at least a meeting
of minds for Maia

Marc will be a good listener
if she decides to talk

perhaps she'll be excited   as I am
by the sudden flowering of our relationship
with earth   pine-trees   pre-Cambrian rocks
water clear as afternoon light

silence   solitude
the rhythmic beat of paddle
cushioned against the side of the boat

the far-awayness

I know how the Iroquois felt about this land
before we took it from them

but Maia's a frosted pillar of salt
pale as the watery thin-lipped moon

one morning there's a bear

we didn't know
till Maia and I were walking back to camp

– look behind you – Marc says
and we turn and see her   backlit against grassland
– don't run   just walk –   he says   – walk very slow –

the bear seems calm   although her cub's with her
but they look as innocent as if they're auditioning
for some cute children's movie

the little one running and jumping
and pulling the fur under her mother's throat

Maia's also calm   calmer than I am
it's a visible danger   one she can cope with

– keep walking – Marc says   voice smooth as breakfast milk

we see trees stripped naked above the beaver dam
mist fingers orchids as if they're everyday

the morning's still as breath sucked in

– keep walking –   he says

a shaft of sun catches spiders' webs slung between trees
joining us all together

these dying birch   this land   this water
this bear and her cub

and all of us   feeling our way
under the patient trees

each day we move through islands of loneliness
loons call in sad voices

lake water clasps and releases us
clasps and releases us

greeting each stroke of our paddles
like the return of old friends

(Iroquois people once ran through these forests
their footprints binding them into the earth)

tonight we're camped by a lake
which looks as if it's set among high mountains
but that's the slippage of history
as the Great Lakes rose and sank and rose again

Marc may not be able to touch Maia
but her face alters as she looks at him

or perhaps it's only the smell
of newly-damp branches of pine

we roast sausages   bake sourdough bread
the Northern Lights reflect
in the evening lap of water on rocks

– it's even better than The Illusory City –
I say to her

if I walk a little way into the bush   and turn
our tents with their beckoning lamps
look like warm pumpkins
more welcoming than any home I've been in

like snails   we've carried them here on our backs

they were light as blossom
without the Tikki Tikki Man

I love to swim in the evenings
in calm lake water
clean as a new melt glacier

as I slip naked into the water I tell Maia
– it's like putting on a dress
made of moonlight –

she's standing by herself in the shallows
but I think she wants to join me
while the men are collecting firewood

I swim up a side creek   pretend I'm a beaver
building his own house for the first time

we start having strange dreams
as if we're at high altitude
our minds drift into places
our bodies can't follow

last night I thought I was a chipmunk
pleased with my new grown-up stripes
planning my nest for the babies
that would follow

my nose twitched with the rich savour
of pine cones and worms

I longed for autumn
so I could gather up mushrooms
put them to dry on the tops of saplings

I dreamt of my family   striped and beautiful
running among birch trees and pine

Maia says she dreams of the wolf
trotting the height of land   like a warrior king

he's made from the earth   he's part of the earth
he's a family man   he has his tribe close by

– I hear them calling to each other –
she says   smiling

his home's a deep burrow under trees
his voice more lonely than any other voice
but   like the loon   he's not lonely
he's at home with himself and his world

the next morning there are tracks
Marc says he must have spent the night
circling our campsite
marking his territory   shutting us in

we slide the canoe into water
so clear we hover above it like gods
feeding on pink and gray stones of happiness

each day our arms grow stronger
as we bend our backs to the business
of easy travel   *glissando*

but when we lift the canoe out and onto our backs
at the portage

our footprints   heavy as giants
sink deep into the memory of last year's leaves
crushing whole lifetimes of insects with every step

Maia smiles at Marc and sometimes speaks to him

on our last night she strips off her clothes
and swims with me

Postscript

among the pigeon towers of Isfahan

on the day a pigeon came to sit on the Prophet's shoulder
tail spread out like the leaf of a sheltering palm

the Prophet's words
floated out to his listeners on a ribbon of music

silver trumpets sounded from the high cliff
so that when the pigeon flew away

everything about it had become an act of devotion

do you remember the evening
we held hands for the first time?

we were strolling among the pigeon towers

phosphorescent droppings gleamed like summer lightning
brightening the roses of Isfahan

how closely those cucumber and melon fields lay together
guarding their cargo of small worlds and singular planets

they shone   you said
fertile and concupiscent as the language of lovers

– il faut souffrir pour être belle –
says the storyteller
as his camel kneels patiently beside him

he absentmindedly caresses one of its knobbly knees
and it lowers its patrician head

– il faut souffrir –
he says again
– pour être intéressante
pour devenir immortelle –

the camel spits so far
its spray reaches the horizon

– you must remember
The Illusory City –   he says

– you must look for the roses
of Isfahan –

and a great wind comes up
and carries them away

About the Author

Caroline Carver began writing poetry in the mid-1990s, and won the National Poetry Prize with a poem about killing a shark in 1998. Since then she has won or been placed in many competitions, winning the prestigious Silver Wyvern Award from Poetry-on-the-Lake in Orta, Italy, and the first Guernsey Poems On the Buses competition. She was Commended in the 2010 National Poetry Competition.

Caroline was born in England, brought up in Bermuda and Jamaica, finished her education in England, Switzerland and France, and then emigrated to Canada for 30 years. Since she returned to England she has travelled widely with her poetry. She's a Hawthornden Fellow, resident poet at Trebah Gardens and very active in poetry affairs in Cornwall.

Acknowledgements

With special thanks for advice and encouragement from:

Penelope Shuttle, Dr Alyson Hallett, Dr Catherine Walters, Angie Stoner, Roz Quillan Chandler, Brigid Smith and, most importantly, Adele Ward.

Recent work has appeared in Agenda; Orbis; Acumen; Artemis; HQ Poetry Magazine; Datura: an anthology of esoteric poems; Mandragora; Alhambra calendars 2010 and 2011; Poetry Calendar 2012 and Poetry Calendar for Young Readers 2012; The Price of Gold (Grey Hen Press) 2012, and WordAid anthologies 2010 and 2011. Prizes and awards in 2010/11 include winning the Guernsey On the Buses Competition and a Commended in the National Poetry Competition. Work has also been published in various online magazines including Michelle McGrane's Peony Moon; Ink, Sweat & Tears; and Abegail Morley's WordPress blog. I'm grateful to everyone who's been kind enough to publish my work and also very particularly to Hawthornden, for the space it gave me.